Looking at theatre

About this book

The world of theatre includes all kinds of entertainment, besides plays. Mime, musicals, opera, ballet and puppets are all part of this fascinating world. Some theatre will make you laugh or cry, some may even frighten you. But, if it is good, you should never be bored! Remember that theatre is put on for you by real, live performers, though the worlds they create may be quite new to you and imaginary. This book introduces you to that magic world of theatre, but does not just show you the stage. It takes you back in time to describe the theatre as it used to be, and also backstage to find out how much hard work goes into putting on a play.

Consultant *J. C. Trewin*
Author *Robin May*
Editor *Jo Jones*
Art Editor *Amelia Edwards*
Designer *Stephanie Pearce*
Picture researcher *Sandra Assersohn*

Curtain up

Theatre can be a famous play by Shakespeare or a clown being hit in the face by a custard pie. It can make you laugh or cry or frighten you. It can be acted, sung or danced, or all three. Turn on the television tonight and you will probably see a play. Turn on the radio and you will hear one. Some people act for a living, others act for fun. But it's all theatre—or drama, another word for a stage play. The word theatre comes from an Ancient Greek word which means *behold* or *see*. Theatre is certainly a spectacle, but it should also be a treat for the ear. Remember that theatre is as much yours to enjoy as the cinema. Turn your room into a theatre or use a field or garden. All you need is an idea. Then let your imagination soar, as playwrights have down the years!

▲King Lear

▼The Merry Wives of Windsor

Armchair theatre

Your sitting-room becomes a theatre whenever you watch a play on TV, or listen to one on the radio. Just imagine the size of the audience who'll watch this episode of Leo Tolstoy's *War and Peace*, which you can see being recorded here. TV also gives you the chance of seeing actors and dancers from all over the world. But just look at the drama you can see acted live on stage.

Tragedy

Why make yourself sad watching grim events on stage? The answer is because it can be an exciting and moving experience. You leave the theatre feeling you understand more of life. The play may be this tragedy of *King Lear* by Shakespeare, about the downfall of an unwise old king. Or it may be a sad story about the downfall of an ordinary person. If it's finely done, you'll care what happens.

Read a newspaper or watch the TV news any day. Tragedy happens all the time and a playwright can transform a tragic tale into gripping theatre. But you need more than just a sad happening to make tragedy really grand. That's why some of the greatest tragedies are about men and women who have everything, and lose everything.

Comedy spells laughter

Everyone likes a laugh and playwrights have been doing their best for more than 2,000 years to keep audiences amused. In *The Merry Wives of Windsor* by Shakespeare, a fat old knight makes a fool of himself chasing two merry wives.

Making people laugh is a serious business and needs skill, both in writing the lines and acting them. There are two basic types of *gag* or joke: those which are vocal, such as funny lines; and those which are physical, like falling flat on your face or bumping into the furniture.

There is often comedy in serious plays. This is because, as in real life, laughter keeps breaking in at serious moments.

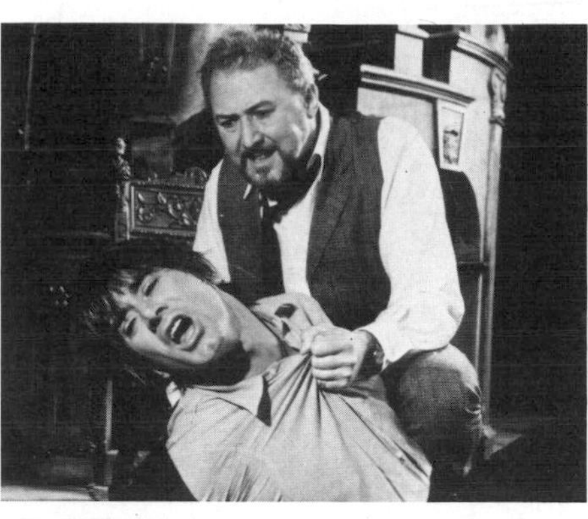

Thrillers

Another kind of drama is a thriller. In some thrillers you have to guess who is the murderer. In others you know who the criminal is, but watch how he or she tries to stay undetected. In *Sleuth* by Anthony Shaffer, the author keeps the audience guessing as to what is really happening.

Acting without words

Mime is a very unusual sort of acting as it's done without words. Every movement of the face and body helps to tell you what's happening. Try some mime out for yourself. First, mime happiness, terror or anger, and ask your friends if they can guess which feeling you are trying to show. Then work out a short play.

Farce

Farce takes comedy one stage further, so that really ridiculous things happen. Some say it's tragedy turned upside-down. Ordinary people are put in impossible or silly situations, like these characters in Feydeau's play *The Lady from Maxim's*. We laugh at the hero's embarrassing situation.

Now read on

There's nothing to beat the excitement of a live audience watching live performers on stage. Imagine you're watching these performers on TV and then imagine them on a stage in front of you, only a few feet away.

Now you're invited to find out more about the world of theatre. So read on!

Children's theatre

What about theatre for children? There are plenty of 'grown-up' plays that young people will enjoy, even classics like *Julius Caesar* by Shakespeare. But playwrights didn't really begin writing especially for children in any great numbers until our own century.
All over Europe, and especially in Russia, playwrights have made a real effort to write for young people. They have based many of their plays on fairy or folk tales.

Firm favourites
In Britain and America, the most successful children's play has been *Peter Pan* by J. M. Barrie. This is the story of a boy who flew in the window of the Darling household and took the children to the Never-Never land of adventure over 70 years ago.
Another famous children's play is *The Blue Bird,* written by a Belgian, Maurice Maeterlinck, also 70 years ago. And *Emil and the Detectives* by Erich Kastner is still a favourite which tells the adventures of a German boy.
But not all good children's plays are 70 years old. Modern writers are producing good, new drama. Excitement really comes over in this scene from John Wiles' play *Agamemnon and the Golden Masque.*

Family fun
In Britain, pantomime is a Christmas entertainment based on old fairy tales such as *Cinderella* or *Aladdin.* But the story includes knockabout funny men, pantomime 'horses' and jokes based on radio and television programmes.
The Principal Boy or hero (Prince Charming in *Cinderella*) was always played by a girl, though men have been taking over the part. And Cinderella's Ugly Sisters are played by men, as they are here!
British pantomime is less than a century old, but its origins go back far longer. For other countries, pantomime means mime, or acting without words.

▼Cinderella

▲Agamemnon and the Golden Masque ▼Ali Baba and the Forty Thieves

Spectacle on ice
Ice shows became very popular family entertainment 20 years ago. These can be pantomimes in the British style, like this one based on *Ali Baba and the Forty Thieves,* or musical shows on ice. The skaters mouth the words which are spoken by actors off-stage using microphones.

The Christmas story
Nativity plays, which tell the story of the infant Jesus, are given all over the Christian world in churches and schools at Christmas. For many children, it's their first chance to act.

Abracadabra!
Finally, there are magic shows, given either by a single magician, like Panzero in the photograph below, or a whole group of them in a stage show. This gives some people a chance to boast that they know how the tricks are done. Most of us, though, haven't a clue how Panzero made his wife float!

Do it yourself
Why not write a play for children yourself? Make sure that there are lots of parts, so that all your friends can join in. The plot or story can be as simple or as fantastic as you like!

Knockabout fun

The greatest show on earth! That's what many people call the circus. Two thousand years ago in Roman times it meant chariot racing and athletics. But, when the modern circus was started 200 years ago, horses were the main attraction. They are still popular, of course, along with the acrobats, wild and performing animals and clowns.

Clowning around

The clowns come on between the animal acts, the amazing trapeze artists and the other performers. They create a splendid world of disaster and insults, their faces heavily painted, their fun fast and furious. We laugh at their lunacies all the more because no one really gets hurt, though everyone usually gets wet!

You can find out more about other sorts of clowns in the section beginning on page 12, for these merry men have tumbled their way through the history of theatre.

A life of their own

Puppets are popular with young and old alike all over the world. Good puppets are particularly fascinating as they seem to take on a life of their own.
One well-known kind of puppet is the *marionette,* like the one in the photograph. This sort is controlled by strings or wires from above. Germany and Austria are especially famous for their marionettes, some of which present musical shows. Then there is the rod puppet, which is supported and moved by rods. A rod puppet can't be moved fast, but can be controlled well and moved very beautifully.

Glove puppets

Some of the best puppets are the simplest ones, the hand or glove type. These have firm heads and hands and loose costumes. The puppeteer manages the puppet by putting his first finger and thumb in its hands. The puppeteer is hidden by a screen, with the puppet acting above it. These lovable puppets have produced famous characters. In Britain, there's Punch, whom you can see beating poor old Judy. Others are Kasperl the peasant in Germany, and Petrouchka in Russia. Petrouchka, like Punch, is descended from an Italian character called Pulcinella.

Never out of date

Puppets have a long history. Statues in Ancient Egypt and Greece and the religious idols of African tribes were made to move their heads. Like clowns, puppets are never out of date!

Song and dance

Think of an empty stage. Add actors and actresses, fill the orchestra pit with musicians and the stage with scenery. Strike up the music and you've got a musical!
Well, it's not as easy as that. Not all actors can dance or sing. Not all singers or dancers can act. It's a big job putting on a musical show. But the result can be entertainment for thousands. Musicals run for years if they are popular enough. That means a good story, good songs and dances and tip-top performers.

Famous hits
A musical that's full of good tunes and good parts for boys is *Oliver!* This is one of Britain's most successful musicals, based on Charles Dickens' novel, *Oliver Twist.*
Many of the best musicals have been American. You may have seen some older ones as films—like *Oklahoma!* and *The Sound of Music*—or hits like *My Fair Lady* and *West Side Story*. Shakespeare's play *Romeo and Juliet* inspired *West Side Story,* but the action is set in a tough quarter of New York rather than in Verona in Italy.
Musicals now have stories about every kind of subject, not just simple romantic stories as early ones often had. The biggest hit of the late 1970s has been *A Chorus Line*. This unusual musical tells how many hard-working dancers audition for a few parts in a new show. It also tells how the director has to make a very difficult choice in deciding which dancers will be picked to star in the show.

▼A Chorus Line ▲The Magic Flute

▲Petrouchka

Acting to music

Opera, which simply means *a work* in Italian, is really a play set to music. Singers perform the parts, for the music is more important than the words, unlike a play. Opera was born in Italy nearly 400 years ago and, especially in Italy and Germany, is enjoyed by very many people.

On a grand scale

But opera has its problems. It's very expensive to put on, especially as a full orchestra of 70 or more musicians is usually needed. In this production of Mozart's *The Magic Flute* at the Glyndebourne Festival Opera, there were 135 people involved on stage and behind the scenes. Also, some singers may have marvellous voices but can't act and may not look right for their roles.

Exciting theatre

The reason opera is so loved by millions round the world is simple. It's often a mixture of good tunes, fine singing, adventurous or funny stories and colourful scenery. These make opera, at its very best, the most exciting sort of theatre of all.

Ballet

Fortunately, ballet is less expensive to stage than opera. And what a lovely world of music and movement the world of ballet is! It can tell a story, like this one about Petrouchka, the sad Russian puppet with a soul. Or it can simply express different kinds of feelings.
The key figure is the choreographer who invents the dance steps. No one works harder in show business than the ballet dancer, who has to be superbly fit. Dancers also need to be musical and to have graceful bodies.

Ballet today

Today's leading ballet countries include America, Britain, Russia and Denmark. But ballet's huge public owes most to a group of Russians living some 70 years ago. A genius called Diaghilev gathered a team that included the choreographer Fokine and the dancer Nijinsky.
Ballet had very often been just a display of pretty dancing. But this team made it into vivid, colourful drama. Now it's a wonderful mixture of movements, music and painting, and as fine as anything in the theatre.

Indoors and outdoors

So you want to go on the stage? Well, it's a hazardous profession in many countries, including Britain and America. There are too many actors chasing too few jobs in the theatre.

Training to be an actor
But, if you are really keen on acting, it's common sense to go to a drama school. True, not everyone does, and no one can teach you to be a good actor if you have no talent. But certain aspects can be taught. The students here are learning good speech and how to use their voices; fencing and acting. Dancing, movement and make-up are also taught. And, of course, you'll have your efforts commented on by experts.
Most young people go to drama schools at around 18 years old—probably the best time. By then you know your own mind!

Acting for fun
Most people don't become professionals, but act in amateur groups. There are thousands of these in Britain alone, large and small. They welcome keen young people who'll help backstage as well as act.
Many schools put on plays in which you can take part.
There's even a good way to enjoy plays set for examinations. You can act them out, or read them aloud in a lively way in class.

Theatre experiments
Actors give all kinds of entertainment like this colourful show in the streets. It's a way of involving people who don't go to the theatre.

▲Voice production

▲Fencing

▲Acting

▼Street theatre

▲Open Air Theatre, Regent's Park ▼Minack Theatre

Workshop drama
On the professional side, more small companies are springing up which give *workshop* productions. These may be in cellars, public houses or make-shift theatres. In big cities some companies perform at lunch-time so that office workers can come and watch. Many do experimental plays, some of which are transferred to large theatres if they are successful.

University drama
Some of the luckiest actors are at universities. They often have fine new theatres with brand-new backstage equipment, especially in America. These are amateur companies, though professionals may be in charge.

Open-air theatre
There are quite a few theatres built in the open air. A famous one in London is the Open Air Theatre in Regent's Park. This is a performance of *A Midsummer Night's Dream*. Many other Shakespeare plays are given every summer rain permitting! New York has an open-air theatre in Central Park, where plays by Shakespeare are acted free. In Italy opera is performed in the open air in the summer. In the old Roman arena at Verona, 20,000 people gather under the stars to watch the performances.
Just imagine you're in the audience watching this performance of Shakespeare's *Othello*. The Minack Theatre at Porthcurno in Cornwall has been carved out of the top of the cliff.

Bring on the clowns!

Clowns must have been playing the fool when our ancestors lived in caves. But the actual job of Fool—as clowns, buffoons and jesters have often been called—dates back to the theatre of Ancient Greece, 2,000 years ago. Later, as the theatre almost died in Europe when the Roman Empire fell, travelling bands of entertainers kept it alive. Their descendants were there when it was reborn in the Middle Ages. Some made kings laugh while others entertained commoners in cities, towns and villages.

2,300 years ago
A Greek masked Fool in a comedy

Around 1350
Animal dancers wearing masks

Around 1450
Fool being tormented by a devil

Around 1580
Italian *commedia dell'arte* play with Pantalone on his horse

Around 1810
British clown Grimaldi, with an actor as the frog

Around 1830
Sad French clown called Pierrot

Around 1850
Scene from a London pantomime

Around 1450
A court jester
with cap and bells

Around 1500
Comic Japanese play
with clowns

When real plays were written again in the 1500s, there were often good parts for Fools. In Italy, there were plays called *commedia dell'arte,* in which the actors made up their own lines. Famous characters—like Pantalone on his 'horse' in the time chart—were born. Some, like Punch, are still alive today. In our times clowns like Charlie Chaplin and Laurel and Hardy have made films. And clowns still make us laugh in the circus. You don't have to wear cap and bells to be one!

Around 1595
Bottom the weaver has
become an ass in
Shakespeare's *A Midsummer Night's Dream*

Around 1630
French clown called
Gros Guillaume
('Fat William')

Around 1600
Hanswurst, a Fool
from Vienna

Present day
Punch and Judy glove
puppet show

Present day
Circus clown and
American Hobo clown

First plays

Many thousands of years before the first plays were written, people were acting very simple 'plays' in steaming jungles, in mountain valleys, in deserts and on plains. Tribes acted out dance dramas to their gods to pray for rain or for success in hunting and war. They performed thanksgiving dances if their prayers were answered.

Echoes from the past

All theatre—plays, ballet, opera, musicals, pantomime, the circus—can be traced back to these prehistoric dances.

Genuine ones are still danced by Red Indians, Africans, mysterious tribespeople in New Guinea and others. Have you seen them in films or on TV? Yes, the theatre is very old indeed! But the theatre as we know it began in Ancient Egypt some 3,000 years ago. Plays about gods were given beside temples in front of vast crowds, some of whom took small parts in the story at times.

The Greeks start writing

We know little about the Egyptian plays. The first great plays that have survived were written and acted in Ancient Greece some 2,500 years ago.

The city of Athens was the centre for playwriting. Greek theatre began as a religious festival in praise of the gods. The audience looked down from a hillside at the actors—the *chorus*—singing and dancing in a circular space called an *orchestra* with an altar in the centre. Next came plays with a chorus and other actors as well. There were wooden seats for the audience and a building behind the orchestra. Later, theatres were built in stone. This one above, at Epidaurus, is 2,300 years old. The first great plays were by Aeschylus (say *Ees-kill-uss*), whose dramas about the tragic story of the hero Agamemnon and his family are still performed. Comedy was popular, too.

Some Red Indian tribes loved bear meat and put bear grease on their hair and skin. Before hunting they danced a bear dance.

A dancer from West Africa, in a raffia costume which covers the whole body, wears an animal-head mask.

More than 3,000 years ago In an Egyptian Temple a priest, acting as the god Horus, wears a falcon mask.

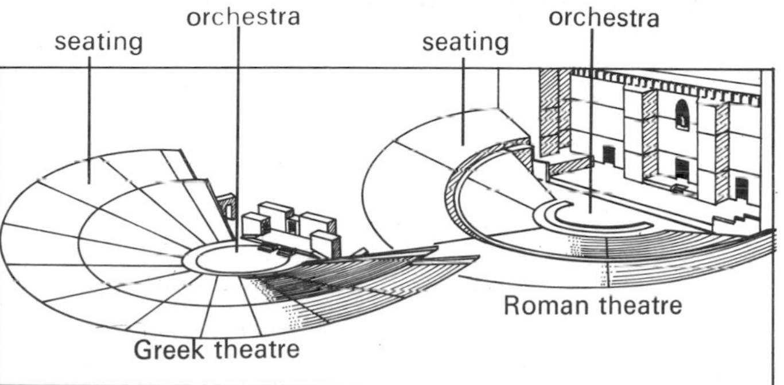

The Romans take over

When Rome conquered Greece she took over her theatre without improving on it, although stages were bigger. The diagrams below show there were other differences. Can you spot them?
Slaves were used as actors and rough comedy was very popular. So were chariot races, a very exciting form of theatre. Unfortunately, blood-drenched shows in the Amphitheatre or Arena were popular, too. Gladiators like the ones in the mosaic at the top of the page fought each other or wild beasts. Both men and women—such as the early Christians—were thrown to the lions. There were also mock naval battles in flooded arenas, where many people were killed.
These horrors ended when Christianity became the official Roman religion. But then even plays were disapproved of. Rome fell to wild tribes and the theatre seemed dead. Only a few entertainers, including singers and acrobats, kept the theatre alive. Some of them performed for chiefs in their halls or wandered around Europe, acting wherever they could.
But in the Far East . . .

Amazing theatres

The theatres were so big that actors (there were no actresses) wore masks. These showed the audience what sort of men or women the actors were playing. They also might have acted as loudspeakers, but voices carry very well in most Greek theatres. Big theatres had trapdoors for surprise exits and entrances.

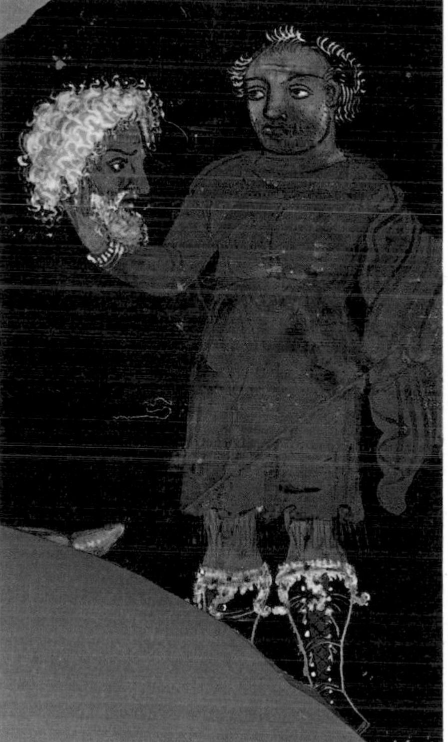

Around 2,500 years ago
A Greek actor holds a hero's mask, and wears the tragic actor's high boots.

Around 2,000 years ago
In this scene from a Roman comedy, the actors wear masks copied from Greek ones.

Around 500-1000
Acrobats with performing bears entertained people when theatre had disappeared.

Oriental magic

Nearly 2,000 years ago, when the Romans were busy massacring people and animals to entertain the crowds, a beautiful form of theatre began in India. It started in the temples, perhaps as ritual dancing performed by priestesses like the ones below. This theatre

was also performed in palaces and always remained linked to religion. Stages were blessed by priests. The players gave dance dramas about kings, queens, gods and goddesses.

The best known form of Indian drama today is the *Kathakali,* which dates from those distant times. Actors—there are no actresses—from Kerala in south-west India dance and mime plays while others chant the story.

Skilled performers

Chinese theatre was established earlier than the Indian, but really became popular about 1,200 years ago under an emperor called Ming Huang. Most plays were funny and were given in palaces, usually by two actors. Gradually, Chinese theatre got bigger. Plays were given in temples, palaces or in public on a platform with a roof above. Until recently, all the parts in Chinese plays were taken by men. They had—and have—to be very clever. As you may have seen on TV, members of the traditional Peking Opera are expected to be experts in song, dance, speech and acrobatics!

Kathakali actors wear rich costumes and heavy makeup. This actor's halo means he is a god.

The heroine of this Chinese play is a man! 'Her' whip shows that she is riding a horse.

In the Malaysian shadow theatre, the puppets are supported on rods.

Colour codes

In Chinese theatre various colours and objects have special meanings. For instance, a yellow costume is for an emperor and red for the next rank down, his official. Waves painted on a banner used to mean the sea. In Peking Opera a black flag means a high wind and a blue one waves.

The Japanese way

Japanese theatre is better known than Chinese in the West, though it's harder to understand. *No* (or *Noh*) plays, which date back 500 years, are given on a raised, square stage. There are two to six actors with a chorus. They are splendidly costumed, often with beautiful masks like the one above. As an evening of *No* can last for seven hours, it is not surprising that a shorter version, called *Kabuki* (say *Ka-boo-kee*), is more popular! There's a Kabuki drama going on in this theatre, painted over 250 years ago. The actors come in either down the gangway through the audience or just behind the screen on stage. The Japanese also love puppets. A type of drama called *Joruri* was created over 300 years ago just for puppets.

More oriental magic

All over South-East Asia you can find traditional sorts of theatre and dance drama which are beautiful to look at. Many are court and ceremonial dances, or mysterious and elaborate temple dances.

They are moved behind a cloth screen, which is lit to make the shadows show up clearly.

The dances of Thailand, Laos and Cambodia are closely linked. Many relate the deeds of their gods.

In the Japanese puppet theatre, the puppeteers without hoods control the most important puppets.

Theatre in the streets

In *The First Plays,* you saw how the theatre vanished about 1,500 years ago, except for minstrels and acrobats who provided some entertainment. It wasn't until 500 years later that the Church revived the theatre. Churches were then the centre of everyday life. Short scenes were given as part of the festivals of Christmas and Easter, with the priests playing the parts. Soon the scenes got more theatrical. Places along the church aisle represented Heaven and the tomb of Jesus on the left and Prison and Hell on the right!

Into the streets

By the 1200s, the plays were becoming so popular that the priests moved them to the streets and market-places. Orders went out that priests should not act, so the ordinary people had a chance to take part.

The plays were presented by local *trade guilds,* who were groups of traders in the same line of business. The shipwrights would perform a drama about the building of Noah's Ark, the mariners, one about the Flood and so on. London's annual Lord Mayor's show dates from this time.

The plays were called *Mysteries,* though in England they were also called *Miracles*. They often formed a whole *cycle* or series of plays, lasting a day. The actors were paid a little money but professional entertainers probably helped out with special parts.

The plays flourished in many European countries for several

centuries, mostly because there were plenty of laughs as well as strong drama. The audiences expected action. The most dangerous part was that of Judas. One Judas actually lost consciousness when he was hanged too realistically!

As few people could read, the plays were in simple verse that could be learnt easily.

Plays on the move

Stages called *mansions* replaced simple platforms. Some mansions were on wheels and these *pageants* could be moved about. You can see a mansion on the left in the photograph of a modern performance of a York Mystery Play. Mansions could be arranged in a circle or placed in a row in the market-place or in front of a church.

Martyr of a saint

This mystery play shows the martyrdom of St Apollonia. It was given about 500 years ago in the open air in France. Can you see Hell-Mouth on the right and Paradise on the left? The spectators are sitting on the ground. Some of those on the upper levels are spectators, others performers. The man with the stick and hat is the story-teller and prompter.

Morality Plays

Two hundred years later came the *Morality Plays,* where actors played parts like Greed, Death and Jealousy.

Bands of strolling players—amateurs and professionals—were performing in the halls of great lords. It was time for real theatres—and great plays.

Play performed: 1547
This painting shows the stage for a Mystery Play at Valenciennes in France.

A mansion represents each scene. There is a very impressive Hell-Mouth on the right. Can you find Paradise?

Around 1420
This drawing shows how the Morality Play, *The Castle of Perseverance*, was staged.

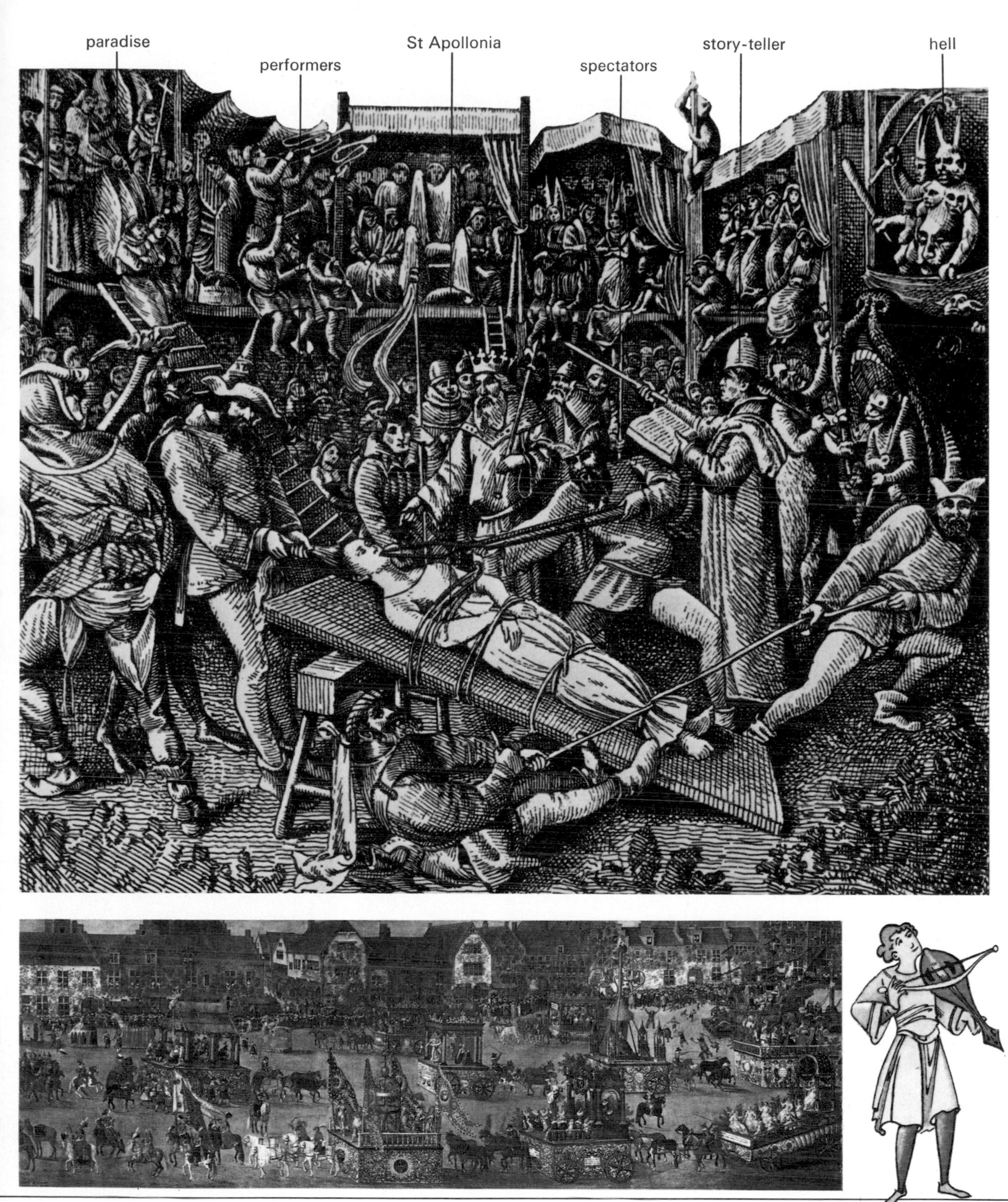

Date of procession: 1615
This royal procession in Brussels, *The Triumph of Isabella,* shows how spectacular pageant mansions could be. The spectators watch each scene as it passes by. Can you see the Nativity scene on the left?

Around 700-1500
Minstrels often sang for their supper in the halls of great lords and ladies.

Back to life

Suddenly, it didn't seem exciting enough to perform religious plays in the streets. All over Western Europe, especially in Italy, people started thinking more about living life to the full in this world than about what life would be like after death. Painters, sculptors and writers began to proclaim the joys of being alive. Some writers and architects started thinking about the theatre.

This exciting period—from around the late 1300s to about 1600—is called the *Renaissance,* meaning rebirth. People looked back as well as forward for ideas—back to the theatre of Ancient Greece and Rome.

Ideas from the past

Scholars started writing plays in the Greek and Roman manner. Or ancient plays like *Adelphi* were revived. This was written by Terence, who lived 2,000 years ago. These plays weren't the right kind to be given in market-places, so architects revived the Roman style of theatre and were soon improving on it.

▲Farnese Theatre

▲Adelphi

Around 1600
Strolling players like this French troupe were still performing in the open.

Around 1580
In the *commedia dell'arte* play on the right, poor old Pantalone tries to win the lady.

Picture-frame stage

But there were new, exciting theatres like this one, the Farnese Theatre in Parma in Italy. Our painting is about 200 years old but the theatre actually opened in 1618. Actors could now use the whole depth of the stage, not just the part in front of the flat scene building. Scenery could be changed and spectacular effects became very popular. There were even chariots coming down from clouds above the stage. Lanterns and candles were used not just for lighting but to produce atmospheric effects.

Parma had the world's first *proscenium arch* or picture-frame stage, which all except the most modern theatres still have today. We watch most plays as if the actors are behind a frame—almost like a play on TV! Unfortunately, except for the spectacles, Italian Renaissance plays were rather heavy going. But luckily a far more popular form of entertainment burst on the public. Remember the *commedia dell'arte* plays, mentioned in *Bring on the clowns*? These plays came from farces acted in southern Italy in the 16th century.

Commedia dell'arte

These words mean comedy of skill, and skill is right! Companies of actors and actresses presented plays in which they made up the words as they went along. Of course, it wasn't quite as simple as that. They chose a subject first, then improvised on it.
You could do the same. Act out, say, the first day at school, or on holiday abroad. First try to remember what happened to you. Then act this out with a friend.

Comic characters

Each player always played the same part. The lovely Columbine was usually the heroine's maid or friend. Old Pantalone, the heroine's father or husband, would try to stop her escaping and the riotous gang of comic servants kept things humming. The most famous was Arlecchino (Harlequin), though Pulcinella, as Mr Punch, was to last longest. Some of the characters were descended from Roman comics, kept alive in the Dark Ages.
The actors themselves were as quick-witted as they were talented. They went far beyond Italy and inspired others. Meanwhile, in England, another style of theatre had arisen and the greatest genius of all was at work.

Around 1580
Two characters dance in a *commedia dell'arte* play in southern Italy.

The age of Shakespeare

It's 2 o'clock in the afternoon of a summer's day in 1599. For the past hour or more crowds have been flocking over London Bridge and by boat across the Thames to the Globe Theatre on the South Bank.
A flag is flying above the theatre to show that a performance will take place.

The play begins
The *groundlings* stand packing the space around the platform stage and the tiers of seats are filled with men and women waiting for the play to begin. A trumpet rings out from the top of the theatre to announce that the play is starting.
It's *Henry V,* written by the Globe's popular resident playwright, William Shakespeare. The famous actor Richard Burbage is playing King Henry. There's little scenery and the splendid costumes aren't in period but the style of the day. The action is fast and there are no intervals. No one present can know that nearly 400 years later the Globe will still be the most famous of all theatres and that the likeable Will Shakespeare—poet, author and small-part actor—will be regarded as the greatest of all playwrights.

Theatre for all
Elizabeth I's reign and the few years following her death was a magic period. For almost the only time in theatre history people of every class went to the theatre, including lords and ladies, tradespeople, ordinary workers and pickpockets! Theatres were as crowded as the bear-baiting and cock-fighting arenas. Many people went to all three kinds of theatre.

How it all began
How did the miracle of great plays, great acting and great audiences come about? The first English playhouse had been built in London in 1576 by Burbage's father. He based it on the inn-yards where strolling players like himself used to act. The English adored poetry. That, together with good stories written by fine writers, created the right climate for a genius like Shakespeare to flourish. You can see below the title page from an early edition of Christopher Marlowe's play *Tamburlaine*. This play started the flood of great plays that followed. Shakespeare was only one of the stars who shone.

Around 1560
Inn-yard theatres like this one inspired the designers of the first permanent English theatres.

Tamburlaine
the Great.
Who, from a Scythian Shepheard,
by his rare and wonderfull Conquestes, became a most puissant and mightie
Monarch:
And (for his tyrannie, and terrour in warre)
was tearmed,
The Scourge of God.
The first part of the two Tragicall dis-
courses, as they were sundrie times most
stately shewed vpon Stages in the
Citie of London.
By the right honorable the Lord Admirall,
his seruauntes.
Now newly published.

Printed by *Richard Iones*, dwelling at the signe of the Rose and Crowne neere Holborne Bridge. 1590.

Richard Burbage: 1567-1619
Richard Burbage, the first great English actor, created many famous roles.

William Shakespeare 1564-1616

***The Globe Playhouse 1599-1613, a conjectural reconstruction* by C. Walter Hodges.**

Shakespeare's Globe
Your guide to the cutaway theatre:

AA	Main entrance
B	The Yard
CC	Entrances to lowest gallery
DD	Entrances to staircase and upper galleries
E	Corridor serving the different sections of the middle gallery
FF	Middle gallery ('Twopenny Rooms')
GG	'Gentlemen's' or 'Lords' Rooms'
H	The stage
J	Hanging being put up around the stage
K	The 'Hell' under the stage
L	The stage trap, leading to the Hell
MM	Stage doors
N	Curtained 'place behind the stage'
O	Gallery above the stage, used by musicians or spectators, and often as part of the play
P	Back-stage area (tiring-house)
QQ	Tiring-house door
R	Dressing-rooms
S	Wardrobe and storage
T	The hut housing the machine for lowering gods, and so on, to the stage
U	The 'Heavens'
W	Hoisting the playhouse flag

The theatres close

We don't know exactly how Shakespeare's theatre looked. Our picture is based on detective work by C. Walter Hodges. Boys played women's roles: the religious Puritans wouldn't let women act. Some plays—including Shakespeare's—were given in smaller, indoor theatres before more select audiences.
In the 1640s, the Puritans closed theatres, then pulled them down. Actors were frowned on by the Puritans long before this. They had to be protected by royalty and great lords or they would have been treated as rogues and vagabonds. The audiences were livelier than today's—noisy in their applause, and jeers!

Ben Jonson: 1572-1637
Ben Jonson was a friend of Shakespeare and a great poet and playwright.

Splendour and spectacle

Four hundred years ago the theatre had been revived as an entertainment and put on in splendid new buildings. Then there was a great demand for equally good shows and plays.

Golden days in Spain
We have seen how Shakespeare and his friends presented plays and how—in England at least—spectacle was not the main concern. Nor was it in Spain, whose 'Shakespeare' was called Lope de Vega. He wrote 2,000 or more plays, 470 of which survive! Spanish plays took place in *corrals*. Corral means *yard* or *enclosed space* in Spain, and it was from performances in such yards that Spanish theatres themselves developed.

Lords and ladies
Meanwhile, far more splendid things were happening at Courts. These entertainments were agreeable ways of passing time rather than great dramas. They were called *Masques* (say *masks*) and were mixtures of singing, dancing and acting. At first all the performers were amateurs. Lords and ladies—and even royalty—took part in them. But the bigger they became, the more often professionals were called in to stage them properly. Stories usually concerned Greek and Roman gods and goddesses and their adventures. The professionals involved became more and more skilled in putting on good shows.

Words and music
Masques were still being performed when opera was born in Florence in Italy, almost 400 years ago. But opera didn't become really popular until the early 1600s. A group of poets, musicians and scholars wanted to recreate Greek drama. This drama was probably *intoned* or spoken half-way between speech and song. In the very first operas, words and music were equally important. But gradually music and song became more important and have remained so. Spectacle was a key feature of the early operas, first given at courts, then in public opera houses or theatres. Both horse and monster moved in this 1638 production of *Andromeda*.

▲**Andromeda**

Around 1582
A modern drawing of a corral theatre, similar to the English inn-yard theatres.

Lope de Vega: 1562-1635
The Spanish playwright, Lope de Vega, founded the Spanish theatre.

Around 1610
The famous architect and designer, Inigo Jones, designed costumes for court masques.

Birth of ballet

Ballet had been a part of masques, operas and plays but came into its own in the middle of the 17th century in France. King Louis XIV, a keen dancer himself, gave it every encouragement. The technical terms dancers use are French for this reason, just as the language of opera (and music) is Italian.
Naturally, artists were in great demand to create the scenery and costumes. Just look at the fantastic costume the dancer above is wearing! This dancer, called 'Watery Phlegmatic Humour', performed in a ballet in Turin in Italy in 1647.
And, because big effects were so popular, artists needed to know a lot about engineering as well. Ordinary people didn't get much of a look-in at these marvels, except in Italy, where opera reached many of them almost from the start. But they had more chance to get to plays—and lively audiences they were.

Here are three examples of Inigo Jones' work. On the left is Oceana, then a Masquer Lord and, finally, a winged Masquer. **These masques were written by Ben Jonson and were performed at the court of King James 1 in London.**

Laughter and tears

In England the theatre was dead. But across the Channel France's golden age of drama was beginning nearly 350 years ago. There, plays were given indoors, not in unroofed theatres, and boys didn't play female parts. Women were allowed to act!

Keeping to the rules
French playwrights wrote plays which obeyed what were called *The Unities*—of time, place and action. This meant that the story of the play usually happened in the same place within a period of 24 hours. Most playwrights objected to this. Shakespeare ranged from Rome to Egypt in seconds in his plays. This is why some French writers, who liked order, considered him a barbarian! But Pierre Corneille and Jean Racine wrote masterpieces using the Unities. Racine wrote good tragic parts for women.

Master of comedy
Molière, Master of Comedy, is France's greatest playwright. He was also an actor and director. King Louis XIV and his people adored Molière, mostly because his characters were so real. He liked poking fun at phonies, such as phoney religious people, snobs, misers (in *The Miser*), and followers of fashion. People who think they are ill and phoney doctors are laughed at in *The Imaginary Invalid.* You can see above an open-air performance of this play taking place in the grounds of the Palace at Versailles in 1674 before the king and court. The Church was hostile to the stage so only allowed Molière to

Molière: 1622-1673
Here Molière plays Caesar in Corneille's *The Death of Pompey*.

Play performed: 1670
The tragic role of Racine's *Bérénice* was played by Mademoiselle Champsmeslé.

Nell Gwyn: 1650-1687
Nell Gwyn began acting at London's Drury Lane Theatre when she was 15.

be buried in holy ground at night. But Molière had the last laugh, for thousands followed him to his grave by torchlight.
France's most famous theatre, the Comédie-Française, was created soon after his death.

David Garrick: 1717-1779
The great actor David Garrick as Shakespeare's King Richard III.

Freedom at last
Meanwhile, in England, the theatre began again in 1660 when Charles II was restored to his throne. Now actresses were allowed, including Nell Gwyn, a royal favourite.

Witty comedies
Theatres were all indoor ones, the most famous being Drury Lane. But the witty Restoration comedies were mainly for the upper classes, not the mass audience of Shakespeare's day. The finest were by William Congreve, including *Love for Love,* acted in a modern production above.
A century later, in the 1770s, Richard Sheridan wrote several masterpieces, including *The School for Scandal,* which appealed to wider audiences.

Theatre across Europe
It was a great age for theatre all over Europe.
In Italy there were riotous comedies by Goldoni, wonderful theatres and opera houses.
The German theatre blossomed, thanks to the Ackermann family and Konrad Ekhof and Friedrich Schröder. And the great thinker Goethe (say *Ger-ter*) wrote fine plays and made the Court Theatre at Weimar in Germany a theatrical powerhouse. All over Europe, too, there were strolling players, performing where they could.
And on a lighter note, the characters of the old *commedia dell'arte* still survived. Pulcinella had now become Mr Punch of Punch and Judy fame.
Theatre was now big business, making millions laugh and cry.

Larger than life

About 170 years ago, at the beginning of the last century, Napoleon and his army were fighting in Europe. The theatre was also in an explosive state.

Actors and animals
It was an exciting but strange period. The same public would revel not only in great actors, like this one, Edmund Kean, and

the Frenchman Talma, in great plays, but also in plays starring dogs and horses. There were even aquatic dramas, with the stage flooded for mock naval battles! And in Britain a 13-year-old boy, Master William Betty, played Hamlet and other great roles to huge audiences.

Romantic plays
Audiences, especially in Britain, had become very rowdy. Larger than life romantic dramas were in fashion. There were major dramatists in Europe, Friedrich von Schiller in Germany, who wrote historical plays, and Alexander Dumas and Victor Hugo in France. And reacting against their extravagant methods was the German Georg Büchner. His play *Danton's Death,* about the French Revolution, seems very modern to us.

Heroes and villains
But what really thrilled ordinary people were the melodramas. These were simple versions of the romantic dramas, full of Heroes and Villains and very little in between except for simple comedy! Audiences knew that in the end Virtue would triumph over Vice and that Villainy would be defeated. All this was acted to suitable musical accompaniment. The working people who filled the cheaper seats were delighted that villains were often noblemen or wicked landlords.

Brighter lights
These lurid plays were given by gaslight, which came in 150 years ago. Electricity arrived 60 years later, and audiences sat in the dark. Before they had been as brightly lit as the stage!

Working as a team
As the century progressed standards of putting on plays improved. The idea of teamwork on stage came from Germany. Before, stars were all-important and no one else had a look-in.
But there were problems. Heavy scenery made for slow action. Lines in Shakespeare's plays were often cut, though by now they were given without changes of story. For 200 years happy endings had been tagged on to some of his greatest tragedies!

Friedrich von Schiller: 1759-1805
One of Schiller's most famous plays is *Maria Stuart*, about Mary Queen of Scots.

Around 1830
In this play from Vienna animals were as important as the human stars!

Famous names

It was an age of great acting, with bigger gestures than today's. The most famous names were Sarah Bernhardt in France, Henry Irving in Britain and Eleonora Duse in Italy. Duse acted more quietly and realistically than either, in a more modern way. Most of the plays were less important than the players, notable exceptions being the very funny farces of the Frenchman Georges Feydeau such as *A Flea in Her Ear*.

Yet the theatre was truly for all at this time, when there were no films or TV as rival attractions. And music hall shows, which were mixtures of song and dance, comedy, juggling and magic were equally popular. In America the shows were called *Vaudeville*. But new writers were emerging, determined to improve the theatre. Let's see how they fared.

Eleonora Duse: 1858-1924
The great Italian actress Eleonora Duse was at her best in strong, emotional parts.

Sarah Bernhardt: 1845-1923
The most famous French actress, Sarah Bernhardt, stars here in *Theodora*.

Henry Irving: 1838-1905
Henry Irving became famous when he acted a guilt-ridden murderer in *The Bells*.

Modern theatre

Imagine a serious playwright's problem 150 years ago when audiences wanted heroes and villains, not plays about real people and their problems. All he could do was write for himself.

The times change

In fact, public taste was changing slowly. The chief figures in the new drama found support from the start, though some of them had to fight hard for recognition.

Two key names are Bernard Shaw and Anton Chekhov, who were Anglo-Irish and Russian. But the Norwegian, Henrik Ibsen, was the real 'father of modern drama'. He wrote brilliant plays about real issues. In one play, *An Enemy of the People,* written in 1883, the subject is corruption in local government. A doctor dares uncover the scandal of polluted spa waters. Ibsen was years ahead of his time, because he wrote also about the rights of women.

Bernard Shaw used comedy to ram home his message, as in the attack on doctors in *The Doctor's Dilemma,* though his masterpiece is *Saint Joan,* about Joan of Arc.

Chekhov brilliantly portrayed the Russia he knew, which was to disappear in the Revolution of 1917. But his plays didn't disappear.

Another great figure in modern drama earlier in our century was the Irishman, Sean O'Casey. In plays like *Juno and the Paycock,* he combined laughter and tears as no one since Shakespeare had done in such rich language. In America Eugene O'Neill towered over everyone; only Arthur Miller and Tennessee Williams have approached him since.

The director

Now the profession of director was born. No longer was the star actor in control, for the director became head of the team. Not that star actors have disappeared—thank goodness! The greatest star actor of the 20th century is Laurence Olivier.

Play written: 1890
Maggie Smith acts the tragic title role in a 1970 revival of Ibsen's play *Hedda Gabler.*

Play written: 1941
Laurence Olivier plays the father in a 1971 production of O'Neill's *Long Day's Journey Into Night.*

Fresh paths

New writers have followed the pioneers. Some have followed them closely, others have made their own revolutions. For instance, the German Bertolt Brecht wanted audiences to think and be politically aware. Fortunately, he was such a man of the theatre that his plays—such as *Mother Courage*—grip and move people.

Theatre of the Absurd

Writers like the Irishman Samuel Beckett and the Romanian Eugène Ionesco have created a Theatre of the Absurd. This reflects what many think of as our absurd, meaningless world.

Pure entertainment

But some shows just entertain us. America's greatest contribution in that line has been the musical. Shows such as *Showboat* in the 1920s started the ball rolling. Other famous musicals are *Oklahoma!*, produced in 1943 and, today, *A Chorus Line*. New plays, new theatres banishing the 'picture-frame stage', shown elsewhere in this book, new young stars, new audiences. Is the theatre dead? Never!

Play written: 1939
On the left is Mother Courage, in a 1977 production of Brecht's play of that name.

Play written: 1953
A 1976 production of Samuel Beckett's *Waiting for Godot*, an important recent play.

What sort of theatre?

Nearly all theatres had a 'picture-frame' stage, like the one above at the Royal Opera House in London. This kind of stage has been popular for more than 300 years, and will go on being popular. But many directors have wanted to bring actors and audiences closer together. Some directors dislike the picture-frame stage behind the proscenium arch.

New ideas
Germany experimented with new ideas in the 1920s and 30s, but it wasn't really until the 1960s that new kinds of theatres were built in Britain. Now you can see all kinds of stage without a proscenium arch. Can you remember where you have seen stages without an arch before? Look again at the Globe Theatre on pages 22-23, and then at the main photograph. There are striking similarities between the Globe and the Olivier stage at London's National Theatre. And the Festival Theatre at Stratford, Ontario, in the smaller photograph, was partly modelled on the Globe. In all these theatres, the audience is seated in a semicircle round the stage.

Variation on a theme
This diagram of the Mermaid Theatre in London shows an open stage which doesn't thrust out into the audience. But the Mermaid Theatre does not have a proscenium arch or curtain.

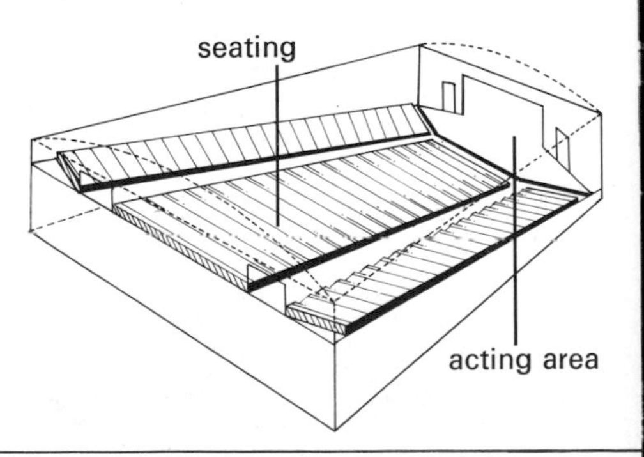

6 6

Theatre-in-the-round
This sketch of the Stephen Joseph Theatre-in-the-Round in Scarborough shows that the seating for the audience is placed all round an acting area with three exits. Some people believe the audience sat all round Shakespeare's stage, too. There certainly have been times before when this has happened. The performance of the medieval Morality Play on page 18 is a good example. Today it's called Theatre-in-the-Round and can be found all over the world. But many more people argue about Theatre-in-the-Round than the 'theatre-in-the-three-quarters' or the 'open' stages which are now generally accepted. The reason why the Round isn't so popular is that often you can't see the faces and eyes of the actors at certain key moments when you—and everyone else in the theatre—should see them. But Theatre-in-the-Round does bring actors and audiences close together.

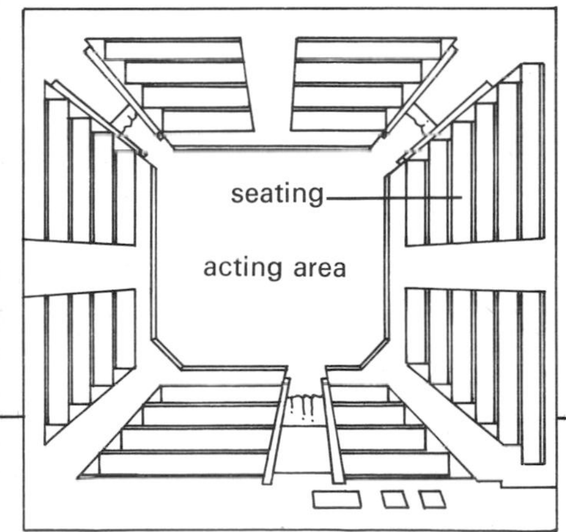

The argument goes on!
The first stage reformers demanded change nearly 100 years ago. This was when the Swiss pioneer, Adolphe Appia, and a Briton called Gordon Craig rejected realistic settings and lighting. Today, television and films provide plenty of realism. There's a strong case for the theatre breaking out of the confines of the picture frame. That is what usually happens now to Shakespeare's plays. But many plays, and some classics, like the most realistic of Ibsen's plays, are best suited to the picture-frame stage. The arguments go on. It all adds to the excitement of the theatre. If there were no arguments, it wouldn't be half as interesting or lively!

Getting started

Theatre begins with an idea in a playwright's head which one day will fill an empty stage. But although thousands of people write plays, only a few reach the stage. You're going to see how Shakespeare's *The Tempest* was put on recently by the Royal Shakespeare Company at Stratford-upon-Avon. Meanwhile, we've invented a playwright called William Shaw whose play, *Death in the Dustbin,* is to be put on in London. If he's lucky, it will be seen abroad, and all over Britain in repertory theatres. These give plays for one, two, three or more weeks, then change to the next play.

Working together
A closely-knit team of people are involved in putting on a play. Apart from the author and the actors, there are two key figures. One is the *producer* who presents the play. The other is the *director* who rehearses it and sees that it is interpreted properly, whoever the author may be. At Stratford, however, there is an Artistic Director in charge, not a producer.
Money to finance the plays comes from different sources. The Royal Shakespeare Company is big and has many plays on at the same time. So public money, in the form of a grant, is used to supplement the box-office takings. William's play is financed by 'angels' who make a profit if the play does!
There are three teams backstage. There is the stage management team under the director. Then there are the theatre staff, who work backstage shifting scenery and looking after any theatre repairs. And there are the front-of-house staff including ticket and programme sellers and cleaners.

Casting the play
At Stratford there's a big company from which to choose a cast, which is newly formed at the start of each season in March. William's cast has to be chosen from scratch. This *casting* is done at *auditions* where actors and actresses show how well they can act. The two stars in William's play don't need to audition as the management knows them well. Stars are hard to get as many are in films or TV.

First, here is William, our Author, with his bright idea. He writes his play and hands it to his Agent.

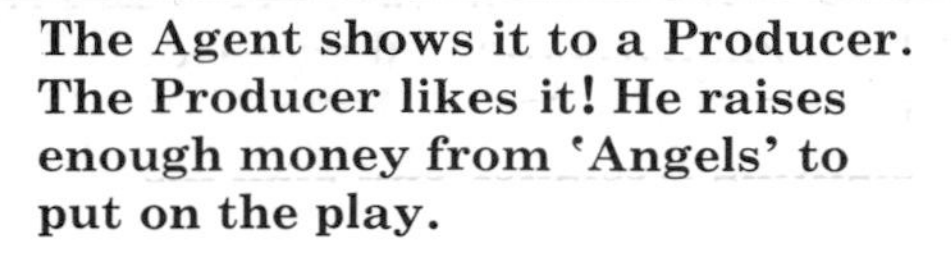

The Agent shows it to a Producer. The Producer likes it! He raises enough money from 'Angels' to put on the play.

Then he chooses a Director. In turn, the Director selects a Designer. She will design the sets and costumes.

Now the hard work starts, with only about six weeks to go before the plays open. Rehearsals begin with a read-through of the play and discussions about the characters. The newspapers are told about *The Tempest* and William's play. Advance publicity is very useful! And now the empty stages are being filled. Many more hours of rehearsal lie ahead of these three actors above puzzling over their moves.

The Tempest
The Tempest takes place on an enchanted island. Prospero, the exiled Duke of Milan, has lived there for 12 years with his daughter Miranda. They were driven from Milan by his brother Antonio. Prospero is a magician and has tamed a spirit called Ariel and the monster Caliban. A tempest wrecks a ship, casting ashore Antonio, Alonso, King of Naples and others. Alonso's son Ferdinand is stranded on another part of the island and meets Miranda. They fall in love. Prospero now uses his magic to frighten those who exiled him and makes them repent. Meanwhile, Caliban meets a jester called Trinculo and Stephano, a butler. After drunken revels, they try to kill Prospero, who easily outwits them. Celebrations take place to bless Ferdinand and Miranda and all ends happily. Prospero gives up his magic, frees Ariel and prepares to go home to Milan.

Planning rehearsals
The Repertoire Manager and the Stage Manager work out the cast's rehearsal schedule.

Voice production
The Voice Director helps 'Miranda' with voice production while rehearsals are on.

Learning the moves
The choreographer watches a movement rehearsal.

The Director also hires the Stage Manager with his team. The Publicity Officer gets to work promoting the play.

Now the Director and cast can start rehearsals. And the Lighting Designer can plan his lighting effects.

Behind the scenes

The two settings of William's play are straightforward and realistic. The designer makes a model of each set, which the director accepts. The scenes are built by outside firms who specialize in theatre work. And after the carpentry comes the painting. William's play has a lighting expert. Unlike his opposite number at Stratford, he has little to do. But the two settings must be realistically lit in a striking way. This means that key spots on the stage will be especially well lit.

Magic at work
The Tempest is a magical play. But the scene backstage at Stratford as it is being prepared has a different sort of magic. It's a mixture of hard work and special skills. While the actors are rehearsing, no time is lost in making these skills work.

Designer at work
The director of *The Tempest* is Clifford Williams. He has chosen as his designer Ralph Koltai, whom you can see above. He's working on the miniature 'wave' that will be added to the almost finished model of the set at the back of the room. Director and designer now agree on the design.

The finished model
This is the finished model of the set, which gives a very good idea of what the stage will actually look like. You'll remember that *The Tempest* is set on an island. You can see the wave breaking on to the seashore, where the action of the play takes place.

Building the set
Blueprints of the ground plan of the stage, which show the position of the set, are made from the finished model. A number of blueprints are needed for the backstage workers including the carpenters and the lighting experts. Here's the huge 'wave', almost finished.

The Royal Shakespeare Company can make practically anything in its own workshops, not just the sets. But props such as chairs are usually hired. Meanwhile, back in London things are rather simpler. There are no magical books to be made. Most of the props will be hired from outside firms.

Actors at work
Now rehearsals have begun in earnest. There are many weeks of hard, fascinating work. Readings and discussions continue. The first *moves* for the actors are *blocked* or worked out, lines are learnt, scripts gradually abandoned. And if an actor or actress forgets a line? The *Deputy Stage Manager* will *prompt* quietly and firmly. Or, as above, she will help with memorizing any lines. The director will be a human dynamo, coaxing, putting forward ideas, encouraging and sometimes criticizing his cast. *Understudies* are chosen to *cover* actors in case of illness. They will have special understudy rehearsals with the stage manager. And the leading actors and actresses may be interviewed by the press.
But some order is coming out of what looks like chaos on stage!

The prop shop
Props (short for *properties* or any items used on stage) are being made in the props department (*prop shop*), which is always kept very busy. Above you can see Prospero's circular magic book being made in the front of the photograph for *The Tempest*.

Special effects

'Take that!' cries the heroine of William's play, striking the hero a stinging blow on the face. Meanwhile, at another theatre, a fist fight is raging on stage, and at another swords are drawn. Of course, all these effects have to be rehearsed very well indeed because the audience has to *believe* what they see.

Bad weather

And what about effects like snow and wind? 'Snow' is usually sent through a *snow bag* hung above the stage. The bag is a long piece of canvas with small slits in it. When the bag is rocked, pieces of paper fall through. The sound of thunder can be made very realistically by shaking a hanging sheet of metal very hard. The best wind effect comes from a *wind machine,* a cylinder with wooden blades in it. When the blades are turned they scrape against a sheet of silk or canvas and, driven at different speeds, it sounds just right! As for 'seeing' wind blowing a curtain, a fan will do it, or you can shake a piece of 3-ply wood. And dried peas or beans revolved inside a *rain machine* with a suitable lining sounds just like rain! But sound effects are often recorded.

Smoke

Plenty of mist is needed in *The Tempest* in the shipwreck scene and for magical effects. Putting dry ice in water sends heavy fog-like smoke that clings low. Or you can put special powder in a smoke box. By warming the powder, you get a good medium mixture of smoke.

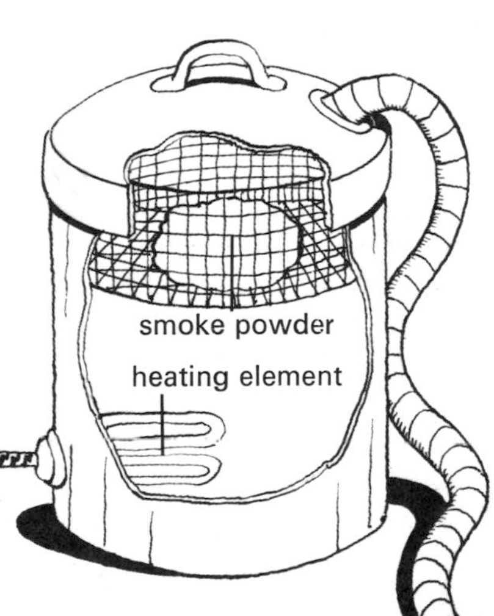

▲The Tempest

▼A Midsummer Night's Dream

Trapdoors

These are just a few trick effects. Others include 'flying' apparatus. In some productions of *The Tempest,* Ariel comes down from the *flies* above the stage, much to the astonishment of the shipwrecked sailors! Then there are trapdoors, which have been used in the theatre for centuries. Can you spot the one in the photograph on the left?

Lighting

Lighting the stage and the actors can be a very sophisticated business. From the modern lighting control board or *console* above, a pre-arranged sequence of lighting cues can be set for a whole play.
One of the best lighting effects is the *gauze*. Shine a light behind it and it's transparent. Shine a light on it from the front and it appears solid.
Magical transformation scenes can be made by this method, also used for mist effects.
In the main photograph you can see the gauze used in *The Tempest* being hoisted into place. On the left, in a set from *A Midsummer Night's Dream,* the 'carving' behind the stairs isn't solid but painted gauze!

Fights

Fights need rehearsing well because they have to be both safe and convincing. A great deal of practise will have gone into this duel scene from *Romeo and Juliet.* Daggers can be real or have trick blades that slide back on contact. And blood can be hidden behind either the blade or the wounded actor's coat, to be released at the right moment.

It's all pretend

Pistols fire blank cartridges, but even blanks burn, so they are never fired too close. Slaps on the face can be real, but the hitter and victim must not be tensed up or the slap will really hurt. Or they can appear to hit but the victim has a hand where he can slap it himself—unseen—with his other hand. And falling down is quite easy! Just relax, bend one leg and follow yourself down.

Costume and makeup

Any designer has to be a fine artist and also an expert on the clothes of every age. And when a director just wants something to suggest a piece of clothing our ancestors wore, rather than an exact copy, that must be done too. You can't put your actors into heavy, full armour, just because you are performing Shakespeare's *Henry V!* You can either construct replicas in a light-weight material or dress the soldiers in striking black leather. This can give a military effect in a timeless way.

Start with a sketch

So the designer has to be very knowledgeable, skilful and imaginative. In drawing these costume sketches for characters in *The Tempest,* he can let his imagination go.

Scenery, too, may either be very like the real thing, or very unrealistic, but eye-catching and full of excitement.

The wardrobe

At Stratford, costumes are made in the wardrobe department as soon as the designer's sketches are handed in. Finally, there are fittings to check that the costumes fit. One of *The Tempest's* goddesses gets help in the photograph below.

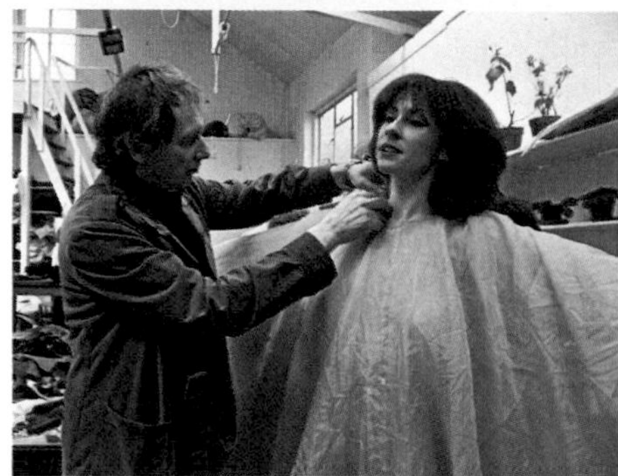

Different styles

Different designers can give a different flavour to the same play. Compare the costumes from two productions of *A Midsummer Night's Dream* which you can see on the right.
Costumes are kept in order by the *wardrobe mistress*. Naturally

Before every performance of *The Tempest*, the Makeup Supervisor, Brenda Ledham, spends 1½ hours making up

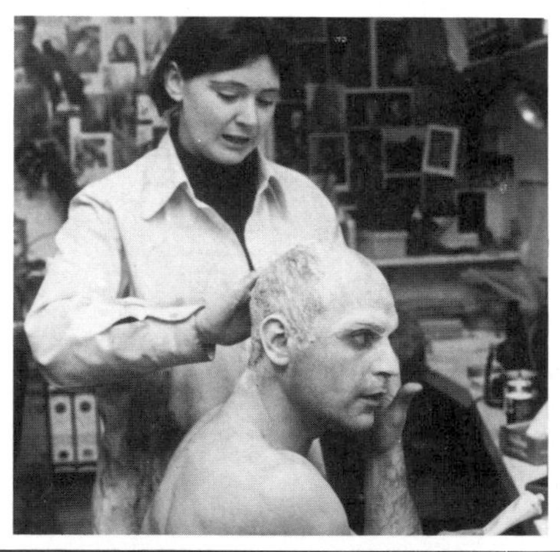

David Suchet as Caliban. First Brenda applies protective barrier cream over David's skin and hair.

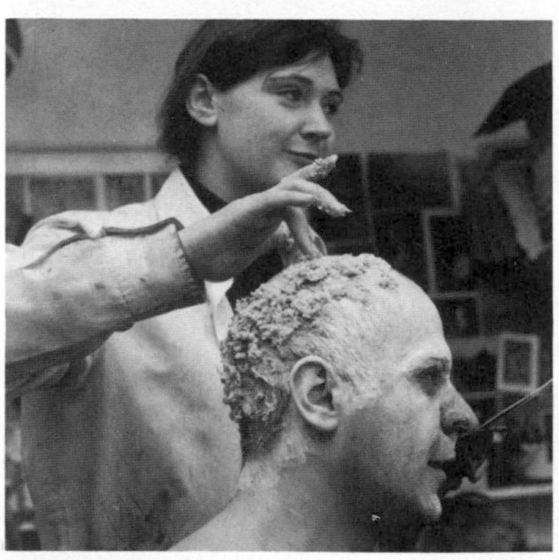

Caliban's false nose piece has been put on. Lumps of porridge, sugar and hot water are stuck on his head!

in a big company there are a number of people doing the job. In William's play there is just one person. The stars each have their own *dresser* to help them change their costumes.
Most of the costumes in William's play are modern and everyday. The cast provide their own clothes, except for the actors playing the two policemen and the actress playing a traffic warden. These costumes are hired from a theatrical costume store.

Wigs
One of William's cast has to hire a wig of flaming red hair, which he pulls off at a dramatic moment in the last scene. But the wigs at Stratford are made by hand, as below, under the supervision of the *wig mistress*.

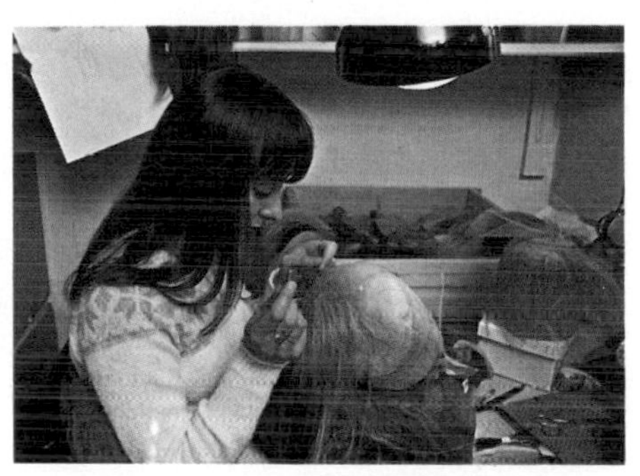

Makeup
Costumes can transform an actor or an actress. So can makeup. Actors and actresses are responsible for their own makeup, but their efforts have to satisfy the director. It's not easy because you have to look as natural to those who sit near the front as you do to those who sit at the back. Imagine the difficulty if a youngish actor is playing old King Lear, or if he has to 'age' during a play!

Of course, those playing 'straight' parts, or characters near their own age, need little makeup, and some wear none. But the eyes especially usually need to be emphasized with makeup, as it's important that you can see their expression from a distance.

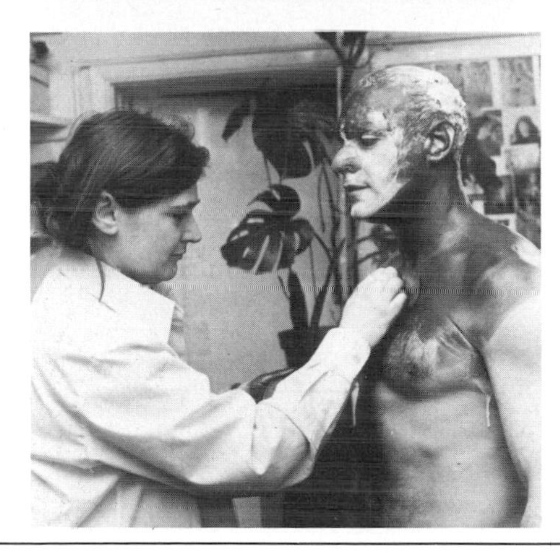

Now Brenda applies one of the many layers of body makeup, to make Caliban's skin really dark.

A thin layer of latex (rubber) is then laid over nose and eyebrow pieces, his forehead and the lumps on his head to keep them secure. And here's the final result. Just compare this photo with the first one on the left!

On stage

Meanwhile, tension is mounting. It's now only two days to the dress rehearsal in both London and Stratford. There are final run-throughs of the play and costume fittings. Technical rehearsals come next. The lights are *rigged* (hung in place) and focussed, and the sound effects are tried out.

Dress rehearsal

Then comes the dress rehearsal. Press photographers have been invited. Things keep going wrong and nobody gets to bed until the early hours of the next morning. A play used to open 'cold', in front of the first night audience and the critics. But now there are usually two or three public *previews* at cheaper prices before the official first night. You might call them extra dress rehearsals, with the benefit of an audience.

First night

The first night arrives! There's an excited hum in the theatre and lots of tension backstage. The actors wish each other luck, the director wishes them all luck, and they do the same to him.

Michael Hordern, as the magician Prospero in *The Tempest*, holds his 'magic' cloak.

Catherine Riding, as the goddess Iris, takes part in the spectacular masque.

The *Assistant Stage Manager* has been warning the actors over a loudspeaker every fifteen minutes how near it is to curtain up. Then it comes: 'Act one—beginners on stage, please!' This is it! William watches his play, nervously. But at the end there are cheers. He goes backstage to congratulate the cast. So does the director. Over a loudspeaker comes a message that the company will be given comments on the performance tomorrow. He's pleased, though, and tells everyone so, but one or two things need 'tightening up'. There's a feeling of relief at Stratford, and the actors and actresses hurry up the stairs to their dressing rooms to change. *The Tempest* has turned out well—in spite of the fact that the lighting broke down, and Miranda stumbled into the set!

After the play
William has to be assured that the audience liked his play. Will the critics like it, too? But it's time to relax. Everyone goes off to a party thrown by the producer, and William goes too. As often happens, the critics disagree. Most say that William shows great promise as a playwright. But one uses words like 'shallow' and 'boring'. But there's already a queue at the box office! Often things don't go so well and plays only run for a short time. But William's writing his next play. And you can be sure that another part of the Royal Shakespeare Company are rehearsing their next play, and keeping the current ones in trim.

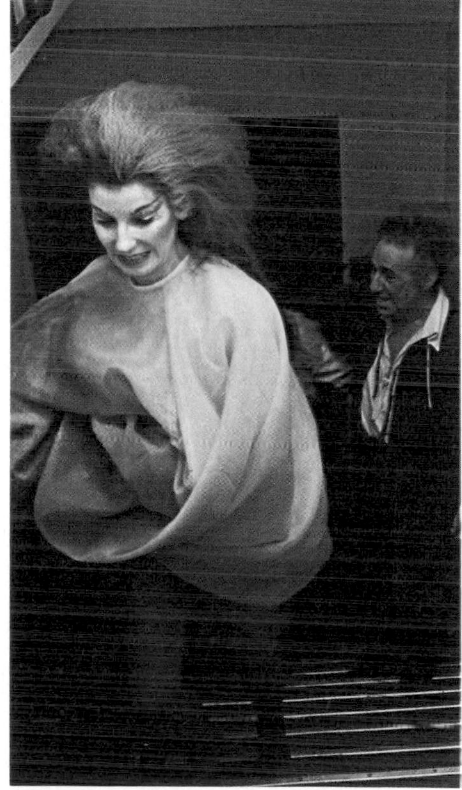

What to do next

Let's take a closer look at some of the ideas about how you can really get involved in acting and theatre-going yourself.
You know already that anywhere —a room, a garden—can become a theatre. But you must not forget your audience, for without an audience there can be no theatre. And this applies to any sort of theatre you do yourself. So give your spectators some help, if necessary, with simple props and settings.

Writing a play
Maybe you would like to try a 'straight' play first, a play with a story. Why not make up the story of *Death in a Dustbin,* the way you would like it to be? Don't forget that a play is usually good to watch when the story moves fast, and when interesting characters react against each other.

Finishing touches
When it comes to props and costumes, your home will have most of the things you need.
But always ask before borrowing anything you want.
Makeup need not be difficult. You may want to study it in detail and, for example, find out how to make yourself look really old. Someone at your public library should be able to advise you on the right kind of books to read. Real stage makeup isn't cheap. You can buy it from some big chemists' shops or direct from the firms who make it.

Mime
Or maybe you'll try a mime. You don't need props for this! What you do need is concentration, but mime can be entertaining for actors and audience. You could have fun by setting your mime in a shoe shop, for example.

Why not improvise?
Do you remember the *commedia dell'arte* plays? All those actors needed was a story idea and they were ready to entertain. And that's all you need. A word or two may do, such as disco, football crowd, the seaside, or the zoo. It often helps to think of an ending to your story first, and to set yourself a time limit.

Pick up tips
A good way to pick up tips on acting and staging plays is to offer to help the local amateur dramatic company. If there are no parts going for young actors, help is often needed with collecting props, sewing costumes or making the sets.
Go to plays at your local professional theatre. Most big towns have a 'rep' (repertory theatre) and some have theatres which put on touring shows. You could also try to get permission from the Theatre Manager to go backstage. Your public library will have details of all theatres in your area.

Become a critic
Have you ever thought of becoming a junior theatre critic? Look in a newspaper for ideas. Don't just say, when you've seen a play in the theatre or on TV, 'That was good!' or 'That was awful!', but write down more exactly what you think. For example: 'Joe Buggins was brilliant as Butch, but as P.C. Penge, Henry Snodgrass failed to realise that the part was a funny one'. And so on.

Theatre scrapbook
Keeping a theatre scrapbook can be fascinating, and it needn't cost a lot of money. Collect programmes, tickets, reviews and pictures of actors and actresses. You could also find out some details of your local theatre's history.
Have a good time!